LIFE
ENHANCEMENT
SECRETS

A BETTER WAY OF LIVING

BRIGHT DESTINY OSAIYUWU

Bible references used:

Nelson, Thomas. (2017) Holy Bible. Nashville, Tennessee:
Thomas Nelson.

King James Bible (2020). King James Bible Online:
https//www.kingjamesbibleonline.org

PREVIOUSLY PUBLISHED
BY BRIGHT DESTINY OSAIYUWU

How To Strengthen the Root of your Marriage

Stressors and Coping Strategies for Daily Living

A Perilous Escape from Africa

Trudeau and the Hunter's Rabbit

Animals in the Volga Forest

This book is dedicated to my beloved family

CONTENTS

INTRODUCTION

THE AVERAGE LIFE expectancy in the world today is around seventy-two to seventy-three years but people can still live beyond that age to one hundred plus years if they are closer to God, make the right choices, decisions and properly take care of their minds, bodies, and souls. However, there has been a significant decrease in that average number over the years which has caused great concern for humanity.

Our lives, and every living thing are determined by God and our time is limited on this earth. Each second, each minute, each hour, each day, each week, each month, and each year, our lives are moving like an athlete towards the finish line or like a candle slowly burning away. There is absolutely nothing we can do about the time that is ticking away because, no matter what we do, we cannot stop the time from running out. However, there are other things we can do to enhance our lives and manage the time we have on this journey.

A person can do many things to enhance and manage their life path and always do the right things, make good choices and decisions, pray to God their Creator and appreciate Him for the time given to them to fulfil their life purposes.

A person can also enhance their lives by applying these teachings to take care of the body, mind, and their soul. The things we do, how we do them, as well as the choices and decisions we make should be the daily basics by which we live our lives. Life's journey is full of difficulties; it is sometimes smooth and other times it is rough, and we adjust ourselves for these distinct phases by doing things that will not further complicate our lives. Life is precious to everyone of us, and that is why it is our responsibility to do certain things to ease our pains and stresses, to make life a bit easier for us all, so that we can collectively live longer lives. There are things that can negatively impact us in life, negative things that can drastically ruin our lives and cut them short if we do not tread cautiously. Everyone should move one step at a time in order not to stumble along the way.

There are other ways we can strengthen ourselves spiritually, physically, mentally, and emotionally to get stronger and happier which will, in turn, enhance our lives. Those things include strengthening our relationship with God; knowing the right things to do and how to manage situations; finding better ways to treat others and react to things; and learning how to take care of ourselves and the people we allow into our personal space. Physically, we need to seek to adopt a healthier lifestyle, get more rest, exercise, watch the food we eat and do the things we love. Emotionally and mentally, it is also important to surround ourselves with positive people, give more of ourselves to humanity; and do simple things like wish people well while worrying less about what is out of our control. By incorporating these life practices into our daily routine, we will make ourselves feel happier, feel better, and look younger. Having peace of mind will create feelings of joy and happiness, and calmness of spirit. It will help each of us lead a life of fulfillment that will enable us to live longer on the earth.

CHAPTER ONE

COMMUNICATE DIRECTLY WITH GOD AND ADHERE TO HIS TEACHINGS

EACH PERSON ON earth is created with the same chances of survival, with the same kind of blood, with the same kind of strength, with the same kind of soul, and with the same kind of characteristics. But as we start to grow in the world, we all will start to form various kinds of life views, values, beliefs, and principles. Our paths will often be determined by how we are raised, and by our diverse backgrounds. Many people adhere to the good values, ethics, beliefs, and principles of life while others deviate from the positive path to sooth their personal negative impulses and different desires in life. Everyone chooses their own path – good or bad because each of us has been given that capability by God. Whatever we decide to do between these two paths is entirely up to us, and the repercussions of our decisions also will totally rest with us.

If we feed ourselves unhealthy food, it will adversely impact us. We should never forget, there is a limit to the things our bodies can take. Too much negative energy can, and will, terminate our existence. Likewise, negative energy adversely affects the mind and soul, and will also determine how healthy we will be physically, mentally, emotionally, and psychologically.

That is why knowing God and adhering to His teachings are of great importance to our lives, because it is only when we know God, and follow His way of life, that we can incorporate the positive practices that will enhance our bodies and purify our minds and souls to allow us to have the inner peace we desire to live longer lives. So, one of the significant things you can do to live a longer life is to seek God first in every aspect of your life, feed your body, mind and soul with the promises of God's words to humanity, and have direct communication with Him. The Bible says in the book of Mathew 6:33, "seek ye first the kingdom of God, and his righteousness; and all these things shall be added unto you," including the long life everyone of us always wished for. Remember, to attain this lifelong request, you must genuinely seek Him in faith, truth and in spirit before He can bestow the grace of long life upon you.

If you seek God first in your everyday life, He will help ensure you have the balance and stability you will need to move forward in the spirit of love, forgiveness, integrity, happiness, calmness, and humility. To do this, you must learn to understand that there is only one true God on earth even though we all have our own unique ways of worshipping and serving Him. Those who believe in God serve Him in different ways. Regardless of how we serve Him, He will always answer and hear our prayers regardless of who we are or where we are from. God does not discriminate between his children; he sees everyone as the same and has given us all the same opportunity to come to him directly. It is important that we never partake in the discrimination of other religions in the world and treat every human being as our sibling. Although, some human beings may be difficult to deal with, but that didn't change the fact that we all are in the same life journey and still treat them nice as God has taught us. There is only one true God. We are all His children, if you are a male, you are his son, and if you are a female, you are his daughter.

We all know that there are prophets, pastors, imams, sheikhs, and other religious leaders who will serve as guides for us, but God prefers the direct encounter. It is best, therefore, that we become accustomed to communicating directly with Him. If you want to experience God's power in your life, you should become used to communicating with Him directly and avoid third party intervention. God understands every situation, and He already knows the things you want even before you ask for them; he just wants you to ask. Speak to your life whatever you want and how long you would want to live, and he will answer you, as long as you are upright in everything you do in the world including properly using your common sense in dealing with situations.

It is sometimes difficult to know those who want to speak for you, especially nowadays. Everyone needs to be extremely careful before using others as intermediaries between themselves and God lest their prayers go unanswered. That is why God clearly stated it in the Bible in the Book of Mathew 7:7, "Ask, and it shall be given you; seek and ye shall find; knock, and it shall be opened unto you." Mathew 7:8 says, "For everyone that asketh receiveth; and he that seeketh findeth; and to him that knocketh it shall be opened."

However, if you feel more comfortable using these representatives to get to God, do so cautiously by making sure they are true representatives of God to avoid your prayer requests misinterpreted before Him. How do you know which representatives are worthy of your trust? It is through their teachings, beliefs, mindsets, truthfulness, behaviors, attitudes, and general way of living.

The main purpose of having God's representatives in sanctuaries and other religious places is to bring God's messages to you, to conduct deliverance for you, to pray with you, and to educate you on how to live a righteous life and find salvation. When choosing a representative, remember: God does not dwell in unclean places and will not work with others who are not straight forward or upright. It is only when they are clean in spirit and upright in their dealings with others, that He will accept requests brought by them. When you look closely at the above Bible verse quotations, all that they imply is that it is best to have direct communication with God. The sooner we understand this, the better it will be for us. Communicating directly to God will not only give us peace of mind, but it will also give us inner peace, better feelings, and the protection we deserve. It will, in turn, give us God's grace to enhance our lives as well as the long life we always crave. So, it is always wise for us to develop the habit of speaking directly to God in order to get our prayer requests effectively communicated to him. Each time we pray, it might seem that God is not listening to us, we may not hear his voice, it all depends on our level of relationship with him; the fact is he hears us always when we pray to him.

There are also other important reasons why you should communicate directly with God. When you have that direct communication with God, you are likely to clearly express your needs and desires to him. You would not want to be in a situation where a representative of God will misquote your requests and communicate those needs wrongly to God on your behalf especially nowadays when some people of God do things of the flesh to suit their own personal and selfish desires.

How are you sure the person you are using as a go-between you and God has a clean spirit? How can a person who is not straightforward and clean in their own spirit success-fully convey your requests and demands to God when they are already discredited by the uncleanliness inside of them?

When you have a direct encounter and communication with God, He can help solve your problems (unless He decides you are not ready for the things you are praying for). It is important that you never feel bad or disappointed if, after communicating with God, you still see no improvement in your problem or situation. Just know that what you are praying for is not what He wants for you.

Sometimes, God withholds a certain blessing just to save you from disaster and other problems that could destroy you. That is the reason He does not answer certain prayers. Simply understand that although it is frustrating, God has set a good course for you. God can also not answer your prayers and will delay certain blessings when He finds out that you are not yet spiritually prepared and ready to receive them. Sometimes God's delay is a sign that He is accumulating more blessings for you. He may come late, but He may come big – never forget that!

There is nothing compared to direct communication with God. When God gets your prayer request directly, He knows exactly how to use it to your advantage; He would not want to give you something that will turn out to be a problem for you tomorrow, or later in your life. There is no excuse to not communicate directly with God. He hears and understands every language in the world, so language can never be a barrier. Your color or race can never be an impediment because God is color-blind. Communicating with God will give you peace of mind. It will boost your immune system, and your entire body system will become healthier and healthier, and you will live longer.

To experience the full power of God in your life, there are certain criteria you must meet.

- You must be upright.

- You must believe in Him.

- You must have faith in Him.

- You must trust in Him.

- You must serve Him truthfully.

- You must accept that He is the only God who created heaven and earth.

Another important aspect of life we must all incorporate into our daily living if our goal is to live longer in life, is adhering to God's teachings and following Him. When we apply God's teachings in our daily routines, we are bound to always engage in the right behaviors, move with the right people and do the right things that will not bring problems into our lives. The word of God is like oxygen that we breathe in to sustain our lives. It is like a life manual that we can all use along our individual journeys.

There are people who are atheists and do not believe that God exists. They do not believe in His word, and they have the right to their own opinion and reasoning. The Bible declares in Psalm 14:1: "The fool hath said in his heart, there is no God". Those who do not believe in God are referred to as fools in the Bible because they lack the ability to know the truth about the creation of human beings. They fail to consider things like the air we breathe, healing miracles, the functionality of the human body and the different inspirations given to humans by God that allow us to manufacture the things we use on the planet today. It is understandable that everyone has the right to believe whatever they choose to believe. They have the right to their own opinions, choices, and decisions but there is lots of evidence surrounding human creation that should make those who do not believe reconsider in order to have a fulfilled life.

Let us go back to review how the teachings of God's words can benefit our well-being and can make us live longer. The word of God is like oxygen to human existence as earlier stated. It gives us hope, strength, assurance, fearlessness of spirit, and a good promise for a better tomorrow. It makes us feel good and calm; we worry less knowing God has our backs. Our fear of the unknown reduces, we move around with confidence, trust and without fear. His Grace upon us allows us to attain greater heights, and our minds are always at rest.

His teachings also show us the difference between good and evil, lead us in the right direction of life and keep us from making wrong choices and decisions that could jeopardize our lives or cut them short. Many individuals today who were not brought up in religious households or who were brought up with religion but did not apply its lessons and daily practices in their lives, end up travelling in wrong direction. They may end up in prison while others get into trouble. Had they followed the word of God, they would not end up in dire circumstances.

When we refer to God's teachings, we are not only referring to the Bible. We are also referring to the Koran and other good religious books, ones that do not support violence, segregation, racism, and conflicts but instead support love, tolerance, understanding, and world peace. These are not the teachings of religious fanatics, and world leaders who use religious teachings to destroy or dominate other people.

Rather, they teach that there is only one God on this planet earth. The only difference is how we choose to worship. When your heart is clean as a believer, and you are always doing the right things in the way you serve God, He will acknowledge you and protect you. God is interested in the good you put out into the world, how you treat others in society, how you positively improve lives, how you positively influence the people you meet, and the positive way you choose to live your life. God wants you to apply the good things he has taught you through the Bible, Koran, and other good religious books to your daily life. God is not interested in your possessions such as your cars, your mansions, your private jets, and other luxury items.

He is interested in our spiritual happiness, and the good things we do for others. Why do you think some rich people, with all the money they have, still feel like something is missing? It is simply because they feed themselves with the wrong ideas believing that what they have can make them happy. They forget that the luxury things they have can only give them temporary excitement and can not make them happy.

All God is interested in is the love you show to others, how you treat people in the world, your integrity and your good principles and values in life. We should treat God's words and teachings like the food we eat and the air we breathe because they energize us. When we eat food, it enriches our body, and when we breathe, it helps with blood circulation. God's teachings do the same for our bodies, minds, and souls.

If we absorb God's words and teaching, we will help others without thinking, and ignite our joy and happiness. Our bodies will function better and we will improve our overall well-being and health thus giving us the opportunity to live longer. The key is to apply God's words to our daily lives, do the right things, assist those in need, and positively improve the lives of others. Only then will we receive God's gifts of calmness, love, happiness, and peace that will make us live longer.

CHAPTER TWO

SHOW GRATITUDE TO GOD AND BE CONTENT WITH WHAT YOU HAVE

ONE OF THE ways we can enhance our lives is by filling our hearts with gratitude and expressing that gratitude to God. Showing gratitude to God for giving us life is one of the things that pleases Him and makes Him want to do more things for us. He is the architect of the universe, and all the things in it. He has given us the ability to choose between all these things He has created in the world. He has made a world that is comfortable for us, and we must be grateful for all the gifts He has given us.

God gave us the ability to choose to be thankful for the things we have, and to be grateful for what we have. Gratitude is a tonic; it activates feelings of contentment inside of us and helps enhance our lives. If we are ungrateful, we begin to develop negative feelings, and attitudes that will be detrimental to our overall health. These negative feelings include grudges, hatred, jealousy, bitterness, anger, grief, and sorrow. Negativity can adversely affect us physically, mentally, emotionally, and psychologically. It can affect our hearts and bodies. Gratitude, on the other hand, makes us happy, and when we are happy, our bodies will function properly.

We must be grateful just to be alive. Everyday, there are people who go to bed, and do not wake up. They die from health problems and natural causes. and there are people who go to sleep without any sign of illnesses or health problems and do not wake up. There are people who left their homes in the morning and never had the opportunity to make it back home safely. They were either involved in accidents that gave them life-altering injuries or other forms of disabilities or they died on their way home. Presently, there are people in hospital on the verge of dying from their illnesses. Others are in hospice awaiting their death. Still others are physically-challenged, blind or emotionally and mentally-challenged. This is beyond our control. The decision between life and death is in the hands of the Creator. It is through His power and grace that we can meet each day.

We must be grateful we are free. There are people out there fighting for their freedom who want nothing more than to have lives where they can make their own choices. There are people who are innocent and yet are convicted of crimes because they were either at the wrong place at the wrong time or were possibly framed for crimes. We have all heard about cases where people are exonerated after serving many years behind bars because of crimes they did not commit.

So, if you are walking freely on the streets today, it is not by your strength; it is not because you are special or too powerful. It is simply by God's grace upon your life.

We must be grateful for good health. It is easy to forget, when our lives are going well, that there are a lot of people fighting for their lives right now in hospitals. They may have money, but their money could not give them good health or save them. That is why we wonder sometimes why extremely rich people still die with all the money they have. There are people with respiratory problems that would give all the money in the world for oxygen just to live another minute. This brings us to the story of a man who was extremely sick in the hospital. He had respiratory problem and was placed on oxygen to survive, so after five days in this condition, he got better with the help of the oxygen. When he was handed the bill, he busted out tears and was crying uncontrollably. When the doctor asked why he was crying, he said that he wasn't crying because of the money; but because of how he has been ungrateful to God who has been giving him free oxygen without requesting for any money all this while. So, if you are alive and healthy, you should learn to be grateful.

We must be grateful that we have nourishment. In some places in the world, people do not have enough to eat. There are people around the world who are suffering from food shortages, either due to natural disaster, bad governance, or economic downturn. Millions of people are suffering around the world today, so if you have food to eat, you must be grateful for it.

We must be grateful for shelter. You may be relaxing at home watching television, with your feet on the table, while others are homeless and need housing right now. So, count your blessings.

We must be grateful for nature and the beauty of the universe. Trees, streams, sky, sun, stars, and the moon; these are natural things we cannot buy with money. They are all free for us to use and benefit from and they are also the things that highlight the beauty of the universe. God did not just create the world. He also created the things that will beautify it to make it comfortable for us. Sometimes, we might experience difficulties and challenges in our lives, but we also enjoy so many other things in our lives on the planet. Instead of constantly complaining about our challenges and difficulties, we should be grateful for other things we also enjoy too and not always those we do not have.

We should be grateful for family. We should be grateful for our families, we should be grateful for our children, and we should be grateful for our friends. There are people who do not have family anymore. There are people who do not have any children at all. There are people who had children but lost them. Those of you who still have your family, your children, and friends around you, have much to be grateful for.

Always fill your heart with gratitude every minute of the day, so that you will experience the full level of happiness in life because gratefulness brings us peace of mind and better feelings that can enhance our lives. Always remember that happy people focus on what they have, and unhappy people focus on what they do not have. When you love what you have, you have everything you need. So, focus on the things you have and be grateful for them, instead of continuously worrying about what you do not have. People have lives that are much worse than our own. We have a lot in life we should be grateful for and should stop complaining about the little things we can handle ourselves. If we are complaining about little things, what do we expect those experiencing worse situations in life to do?

Now, let us look at the scriptures. God did not promise us that there will not be challenges and difficulties in our lives. Instead, He offered those who believed and trusted in Him strength, and the ability to deal with these challenges when they arise. Life itself is already complicated, so troubles are bound to happen to us anytime, any day. The good news is that there is a God who is standing behind us and giving us the strength to deal with various negative situations. Simply knowing God does not make you an exception in this regard. Everyone will experience challenges in life if they are a living being.

Anytime you are in a tricky situation, be grateful for it because there are people out there whose conditions are worse than yours. A life with God does not mean you will have no troubles. It means He will always be there to help you through them. Never assume you have the biggest or worst problems in life because other peoples' problems started from where yours stopped. If you are going through a depression, be grateful. If your business is not meeting your expectations, be grateful. If you are going through a tricky situation, be grateful. Just be grateful in any situation you find yourself in because there are people who never have the opportunities in life that you have now.

When you negatively react to your predicament, it triggers your negative mood, and when you are in a bad mood, it affects your ability to think straight. When you do not think straight, you will make bad decisions that will take you in the wrong direction and will make your life more complicated. Gratitude brings calmness, relaxation, happiness, joy, and good feelings that will positively impact your well-being. When you fill your heart with gratitude, it gives you the feelings that reduce your blood pressure and your vulnerability to other health challenges. Anytime you feel gratitude in your heart, it boosts your immune system and makes you stronger.

We will only achieve inner peace when we are content with whatever we have in life. When we are content with what we have, we worry less, and we feel better. To be content with what we have is to get that satisfaction from the little that we have. No matter what we have, there are still people out there who do not have as much what we have. Not being content with what we have leads to unhappiness, grief, sadness, anger, anguish, jealousy, hate, pains, low self-esteem, and awful feelings. It can ruin your mood, and your entire day. Each time we are not satisfied with the things we have, we become bitter, and that bitterness will affect everything we do in our day-to-day lives.

Discontentment can get you in serious trouble if you continue to be affected by it. Discontentment will make you crave things and will make you greedy. When you become greedy, you will want to get more at all costs. Sometimes your greed will blind you and leave you exposed to danger. Greed can make you desperate, and when you are desperate, your ability to tread cautiously will diminish. That is why you see people engaged in dubious activities just to satisfy their cravings for more of the things they already have. Never let greed for what you see in the world, or on social media, guide your thoughts. Learn to be content in your day-to-day living.

Contentment brings peace of mind, and peace of mind will make you live longer because you will worry less. Discontentment and greed will make you desperate and careless and cause you trouble you will later regret. If you are discontent, you will not be satisfied, and you will look for every possible avenue to fulfil your greedy desires. That is not healthy and may be detrimental to your well-being.

Having the right mindset is key to becoming more content. Sometimes, our mindset is positively or negatively impacted by the environment in which we live, things we see, and the people we associate with. That is why it is imperative to observe the people that are close to us so that we know what they think and how they reason. When we associate with people who are never content with what they have, we subconsciously begin to exhibit similar behavior patterns without our knowledge. People in our lives matter when it comes to the issue of contentment. The good life we create inside of us is better than the one we create outside. You should learn to create an authentic life that feels good on the inside, and do not try to create one on the outside just to impress others. Always remember that when you love the things you have, you have everything you need in life. Contentment is one of the positive attributes we must possess in order for us to live a happier, joyful, and fulfilled existence that will elongate our lives.

CHAPTER THREE

LOVE MORE AND DO NOT CARRY HATE IN YOUR HEART

LOVE STANDS FOR peace, unity, happiness, togetherness, and better feelings. Without love, there is no way we can achieve the things I have described in the last chapter. When love enters places, it brightens them up and makes them better. Love is strong and when we identify ourselves with it, it will linger on with us wherever we go. When we love the things and other people around us, we are positively building ourselves into better people for the benefit of society. It is only love that builds and adds value to things and does not destroy. Anyone who lacks love in their life will certainly lack all the things mentioned earlier, the things that make life more livable.

There are so many things that come with love; love makes us feel good, it brightens our day, it brings out the best in us, it makes us go the extra mile for people. Love is beautiful, love is kind, love has the power to open any door, love brings peace in the society, love unifies people, love brings happiness, love brings togetherness in the world, and love can do many other positive things for you. All these things associated with love will give you the inner peace that will make you live longer.

Before you love anyone or anything, it is important to love yourself. Anyone who does not love what is inside of them, or their own spirit, cannot wholeheartedly love someone else. It is only when you have love within yourself that you will have love to give to others. We also need to learn to do the things we love (as long as they do not negatively interfere with other people's progress or their happiness).

When we do the things we love, we derive joy from those activities. They help us relax and give us peace of mind and make our lives more enjoyable. If you love walking outside, do it more often. If you love dancing, do it more often. If you love playing soccer, football, basketball and other sports, do them more often. It is only when we do the things we love that we can feel their positive impact in our lives. There are people who do jobs they do not really like just because they get paid. They go to work everyday unhappy, not loving what they do, forgetting that when people are unhappy, they have negative feelings that can control their entire bodies.

The impulses from those negative vibes will start to shape the way those people interact with their families, colleagues, and other people in the society. The negative impact that comes with not loving what you do affects not only you, it affects everything and everyone around you.

Think about this; when you do not love something, you get upset about it, and when you get upset, it adversely impacts the way you look at the task or the object. When you are in a negative mood, you make bad decisions. One wrong decision can ruin your day, and leave you with feelings of agony, regret, and sorrow. These feelings can affect your body and make you more vulnerable to health challenges. In order to avoid agony, regret and sorrow in our lives, we should avoid all activities that will invite them in. Agony and sorrow lead to worries and worries makes us uncomfortable.

When we are uncomfortable, we become restless, and when we are restless, we invite stress into our lives. and everyone knows that stress can lead to early death. Lack of love in our lives will only bring us more pain and problems. When we lack love within ourselves, we experience negative emotions such as anger, self-hate, self-doubt, and disarray. Negative feelings do not add positive value to our lives. Rather, they steal from our lives, and impact how long we will live. You should learn to love things that are pleasing to you and add value to your life. By loving those things that give you joy, you will shape how happy and fulfilling you will be in life. You must first develop love within yourself and shower it on yourself before you can extend it to others. You cannot give what you do not have.

If you do not have love inside of you, there is no way you can give what you do not have to other people. When you immerse yourself in love, it enriches your body and makes you feel younger and healthier. It makes your skin to glow and it energizes and protects your internal organs allowing them to withstand every potential negative attack from the food you eat and other things in your environment. The more we love, the better our world will be. and the more we love ourselves, the better our health will be.

Another path to an early grave is keeping hate in our hearts against others. When we hate other people or things around us, we are destroying ourselves because hate only destroys and does not build. There are those who live their lives consumed by hate. Unfortunately, hate can shorten their lives and make people in their twenties look like those in their forties or even fifties.

Hate does not stay in people's hearts alone. It also causes bitterness, envy, jealousy, unforgiveness and other negativities that can reduce a person's life if they are not careful. These negative feelings can cause problems for people. One of the best practices anyone can engage in to live longer in life is to learn not to carry hatred in their hearts against anyone regardless of the wrong others have done to them.

According to some life interpretations, love is light, and hate is darkness. Why live in the dark when you can live in the light? Only love can improve our lives, so we should always choose love which is the only thing that can give us the peace of mind that will enable us to live longer. Hate can reduce the life span of any individual who keeps it in their heart for too long. Hate is responsible for many disasters and negative practices happening around the world today. Hate leads countries to fight other countries, groups to fight other groups, people to fight other people. The root of animosity is hate.

The definition of hate is to feel strong aggression towards another, and to possess a negative spirit of dislike against an individual or group of people, for whatever reason. A person who hates does not want to have anything to do with people anymore. These practices are what are causing various problems in the world today. For example, people hate others based on their color, race, ethnicity, religion, and class.

The fact is we are all human beings made by God to live on earth just like others, and there is no point carrying hate for other people. The best way to address the issue of people who have terribly wronged you to the extreme is to let them know what they have done and how hurt you are. If they apologize for their wrongdoing, accept their apology, and let go. This will free your heart from resentment. If they refuse, or choose not to apologize to you, still let it go, so you do not allow the bad behavior of one person to affect your day, or your life. Each time you are upset about something, it makes you to subconsciously react to things or people around you negatively. and if you are not careful, you could land yourself in a deeper mess and with problems that could ruin your life.

There are reasons why people choose to hate. People hate others who have different skin colors. Others hate them because they do not like what they have heard about them from another person. Always remember, you can misinterpret something you may have heard from a third party. So never use the things you hear about people against them. Always give them the benefit of the doubt by hearing their side of the story. Additionally, regardless of race, color, ethnicity, class or negative information about others, hate is not a good thing to carry in the heart. Just because you do not like someone does not mean they are your enemy, and you should hate them. If your instinct or intuition does not permit you to get close to someone, that does not mean you should passionately hate them.

When you constantly carry hate, it is like placing a heavy load on your heart. When the weight of the load continues to remain on your heart, it reduces its functionality. When that happens, various health issues will start to emerge and can place you in a dangerous health situation that could jeopardize your life. Our hearts are very fragile and there are limits to the things they can absorb without any negative reaction. When hate fills your heart instead of good things, it can affect its performance and cause heart palpitations, heart attacks, high blood pressure, and reduce the potency of your body hormones which will can lead to even more health challenges. You may notice each time you bump into someone you hate that your heart will skip and start racing more than normal.

Those reactions are not in the best interest of your heart because the sight of that person you hate is causing it to react negatively any time you see them. If those negative triggers continue to happen to your heart, you are likely to develop critical heart problems that could end your life. So, we all must try our best to love more and hate less in our everyday lives in order to live longer and to fulfill our dreams, visions, aspirations, and purposes in life. As the singer Lucky Dube once sang in one of his hit songs, we may be assorted colors, but we are all one people.

CHAPTER FOUR

TAKE TIME TO REST AND DO NOT WORRY TOO MUCH

IN LIFE, ONE of the things that can positively boost our hormones and improve our overall health is when we get enough rest. Rest is an essential part of human life, and that is why we relax, and sleep after a long day out or after work. When we do not get enough rest, our bodies will start to malfunction or shut down during our daily activities. It will affect our behavior, and we will not be able to think straight anymore. People around us will notice this, and start to see us as miserable people.

If you do not get enough rest, it will show on your face, and that is why you should rest as often as you can. It is easy to spot people who lack proper rest everyday on our streets, in the mall, on the buses, and in other public places. They react negatively to the smallest things. When a person lacks proper rest, it affects their day-to-day living in an extremely bad way. They become tired, frustrated, angry, irritated, and bitter towards everything around them. It affects their tone, their body, and how they respond to other people around them. Rest is not something we should skip or avoid taking because it is very, very essential to our well-being and our overall health. It is only when we try to skip rest that our good health will start to diminish. That is why you see some people falling asleep at workplaces, while sitting, while standing, and even while behind the wheel.

Lack of sleep is responsible for lots of car crashes and other accidents, and injuries and fatalities. Whenever you do not take enough rest after working for an extended period, your entire body system will start to shut down. This is not something you control on your own; it automatically kicks in once you go past the limit your body can take. We often see drivers change lanes without signalling, while others cut off other drivers. People drive faster just to get home because they are so exhausted. They ignore weather conditions, turn sharply, and commit other road violations which can cause fatalities. The importance of proper rest can not be over-emphasized because it is so essential to our well-being.

You should learn to take care and put your health first before other things in life. You can buy houses, clothes and cars but you cannot buy good health. The only thing money can do for your health is to control it for a specific or extended period; it can not make you completely restore your health once it starts to deteriorate. That is why we should be cautious about how we treat our bodies, minds, and souls because good health is vital to making our hormones stronger and strong hormones fight potential attacks on our health.

Let us all learn to avoid the things that will make our health deteriorate and commit ourselves to doing everything we can to feel stronger and healthier. We should learn to balance our work time with our rest time in order to get the best out of ourselves. When you are doing anything at home or outside the home, sit when you need to, sleep when you need to, take a break when you need to. The bottom line is to get enough rest to respond to your body's needs. As we work to take care of our bills, our families, and other essential things, we should also consider taking enough rest in between in order to balance our lives. We should never prioritize money over our health, and we must accommodate rest time for us to function properly. People will argue that they must get two or three jobs and work extremely hard to keep up with family responsibilities. There is nothing wrong with taking care of family expenses, but you should also remember to take time to re-energize yourself physically, emotionally and psychologically. Family can share your house, cars, clothes, and other luxury things with you. The only thing they cannot share is your illness and deteriorating health, so you must guard your health as you work to provide for them.

You can suffer from chronic illness if you do not pay attention to good health and rest. It can affect your limbs, joints, and other vital organs. The results of chronic illness can be devastating, and can leave people bedridden, in terrible pain, and confined to wheelchairs. According to one story, a man who was limping went out with his family and could not walk as fast as other family members. They were embarrassed by the person and did not want to be around him. This scenario is very heartbreaking to a person with a disability, knowing that those he sacrificed for turn out to mock him. This is not to discourage anyone from working to take care of their families; it is simply advice to people to balance their work and family life and to pay close attention to their health while working to take care of their families.

Lack of rest can negatively impact the organs in our bodies leading to chronic illness. This is not to say that it is only lack of rest that can result in health problems. There can be natural causes that can bring about illnesses in your body. But when we do not rest or sleep when we need to, our brains, our hearts, our blood circulation and our vital organs will start to malfunction, and this will negatively impact how we respond to the people around us. The way we approach people will change. Our sense of reasoning will change, our body language will change, and we will start to see things in a more negative way. Negativity can spread to those around us; it places us in a position that will get us in more trouble and may further complicate our lives. We need to take action to ensure our lives do not spiral out of control.

Always learn to do things at the appropriate time, and when necessary. When we fail to do this, we will unknowingly put ourselves in tight corners, and adversely affect our overall health. For example, a man buys something he is not ready or able to financially accommodate, and as a result, he will be forced to work extra hard in order to pay for the item. It may take years before he is able to pay the bill, and he will have to sacrifice his ability to rest.

Work is essential in your life, but you should also make your rest time essential, too. People may say that they are young, and that a lack of rest will not affect their health. On the contrary, age does not really count when it comes to resting. Each body has a limit to what it can take daily. Imagine working for hours without breaks in-between! That would be extremely exhausting. It does not matter if we are young or not, we should always rest when we need to. When we are young, our young bodies may be able to tolerate excessive loads of work but only for a certain period. We may not feel the impact at the time we are young, but by the time we grow older, our bodies will become weaker and weaker and we will require more rest than we did when we were younger. As we grow older, we will require more rest and we must do everything possible to rest as often as we should.

Many people think it is only our hands and legs that need to rest; but our brains are vitally important to the body's operation. The brain sends signals to our body parts to make them function properly. Let us look at it this way: before we move our hands, lift our legs, talk to people, eat food, wear clothes, and before we do everything, we must think about them first. So, our brains do more work than most parts of our bodies, and the only sure way to re-energize the brain is to shut it down through sleep because sleeping is a vital part of rest. So, when we relax and rest the way we should, the mental, emotional, and psychological aspects of us will be at peace and will make us physically stronger to deal with our everyday lives. When we lack rest, we begin to experience health challenges that will jeopardize our lives.

Another thing that is detrimental to our health is worrying about the things we can not change in life. Worrying about things in life has abruptly ended so many lives in our society today. Worry comes with so many negative things that could affect our physical, mental health, and destabilize us from reaching our goals and potential in life. When we worry, we imagine things in our brains, and mentally dwell on those things. Worry can trigger difficulties and anxieties which can adversely affect our well-being. Most of the things we worry about are imaginary, and are likely not to happen at all, but because of our human nature and ignorance, we still worry about them. Worry can cause catastrophic health problems in our lives if we continue to give in to it.

Each time we worry about things, our minds skip, our body temperature goes up, our blood pressure rises, our heart rate increases, and our ability to think straight reduces. There are things that can happen to our bodies and souls when we worry about things we cannot control. Worrying can adversely affect how we function in society. It can become the root of depression when we dwell on it for an extended period of time. When we worry constantly, we can develop a hypertensive condition that may lead to a more serious health condition which could endanger our lives.

As humans, we constantly crave things we do not need. For example, let us say a man wants a bicycle, and he eventually gets the bicycle. As soon as he has that bicycle, he decides he wants a motorbike. After a while, the motorcycle will not be good enough, so he wants a car, then a house, then a more expensive car, or a private jet, then maybe a new model of the jet. He knows a newer model will not be any better, but he still wants one. This is an extreme example, but it is here to illustrate that people will continue to want more things even if they do not need them.

Human nature is all about I want this, I want that, and people are not often satisfied with the things they already have. The more we want, the more we worry and this can make us develop chronic health problems that may reduce our life spans. It does not have to be that way. We can choose to worry or not. There are people who worry about things they can't even afford. They stress themselves out over something that is unattainable. Worrying about things you cannot have can impact on your well-being and make you develop health problems that will affect your life.

God has given everyone a choice. They can open a Pandora's box by choosing to worry about things they cannot have. Or they can choose to stop worrying about things that are beyond their reach. Everyone has that power. Here is another example. A man says when he gets married, he will not worry about anything anymore. and yet, as soon as he gets married, he worries about having a child. As soon as he has a child, he worries about his child welfare and how he will send the child to school. When he is successful sending the child to school, he starts worrying about the child's grades. After he is satisfied with his child's grades, he worries about the friends the child keeps.

Worrying about everything can be a vicious cycle. There must be one thing or the other to worry about in life. People worry about sick family members, food to eat, joblessness, relationships, family liabilities, and other things. But that is their choice. Every human being may be designed to constantly think and assume how things will play out around them. That is the way we are, that is the way we think, and that is the way we see things. It is human nature. But we all have the capacity to choose whether to worry or leave things the way they are.

Ironically, most things we worry about in life will not happen at all. and if they do happen, the circumstances are beyond our control. So why worry? All it will do is make you sick. Here is a better strategy. When something is bothering you, just keep calm and silent, and allow things to work out the way they are destined to be in your life. Most times, letting things play out naturally will not only save you from unnecessary worry and stress, but it will also give you strength and prepare you for the days ahead. So, the less we worry about things we can not control, the better for our immune system, our ability to think, and our overall well-being. That in turn will help us lead a happier longer life.

CHAPTER FIVE

FORGIVE THOSE WHO WRONGED YOU TO FREE YOURSELF MENTALLY

PEOPLE IN THE world today are trapped and living in pain because of what others have done to them in the past. There have been cases of people still suffering and languishing just because they refused to let go of what others did to them. Everyone of us should learn to let go of grudges and resentment in our hearts against the people who have in one way or another wronged us. When we harbor these resentments in our hearts, they will take away the better parts of us, bring us more pain, and make us function less in our day-to-day lives and activities.

It does not make you a weak person to let things go. It will make you stronger because a strong person understands they have the power to take a deep breath and walk away.

How is that possible? When you are able to control your emotions, you are indirectly controlling your physical self.

Letting things go from your heart comes from the emotional part of you. That is why when you are emotionally drained, it affects your entire physical body. When you allow those negative emotional vibes to dwell within you, they will gradually invite in more health problems. When you let negative emotions go and forgive the wrongdoers, peace and calmness will take over your entire body system. The inner peace you feel will strengthen your immune system making you feel strong and impregnable, and your body will be able to resist illness.

There are health benefits that come with forgiveness and allowing grudges and resentment to leave your heart. At the same time, there are grave health consequences when you refuse to forgive and let go of these things. When you let go of anger and resentment, you will feel a calmness of spirit, you will be able to do things without feeling emotional pain, and you will have the ability to be around those who have wronged you without feeling anger or bitterness. The best of all, you will be able to protect your health. You will also feel happier and enjoy the things you love and be able to be who you really are. All these things will boost your energy and make you live longer on earth.

If you cannot forgive those who have wronged you, you will suffer from unhappiness, bitterness, pain, agony, and many other negative vibes that could lead to high blood pressure, heart failure, heart disease, palpitation, reduced body immune strength, and the breakdown of your physical and emotional health. It could lead you to an early grave.

Harboring resentments against others can make you age faster. You will see the effects in the mirror: frown lines, crow's feet, and ugliness. If you have a constantly troubled spirit, you can subconsciously transfer your aggression to your loved ones and the people around you. You will feel less confident.

Many individuals fear that letting go of the wrong committed by another person will mean they have to accept the wrong doers back in their lives and allow them to be closer to them again. But it is up to the individual to choose whether to associate with them. They do not have to. Sometimes, bringing them back into your life is like giving them an extra bullet to fire at you. There are things that happen to us for a reason, even negative things. We can learn from even the most negative experience. Not everyone is meant to remain in your life until eternity. People come into your life for different reasons. People are there to teach you a lesson, they are there to add to your life, or to take from you, they are there to show you the way. Some will help you achieve your dreams while others are there to try to destroy you. It is your job to figure out their place in your life, and to decide whether to let them remain or to let go. It is your choice.

Letting things go from your heart simply means that you are no longer irritated by the presence of those who wronged you. You can still do good things for them regardless of their behavior towards you. You can point out to them that there is danger to them if they are about to get in trouble, and you can wish them well despite your differences with them. When you do these things without any vengeful spirit, peace, joy and calmness will encompass your whole being.

But there is one thing you must do. You must draw a boundary around them to protect yourself from hurt. If you can do this, and incorporate it into your life, you will never again feel resentment or animosity in your heart towards those who have wronged you. Remember, anger will take over your heart, and will constantly cause you bad feelings that will ruin your days and nights and bring out the worst in you. When there is anger and unhappiness in your spirit, there will be no room for happiness to reside in you. Animosity, anger, and resentment must leave your body first before peace and happiness can dwell inside of you. Positivity and negativity cannot exist together; one has to leave before the other can stay. Allowing all these negative feelings to pile up inside of you will do more harm than good. So, letting them out and creating space for peace will bring you good health benefits.

You must choose between harboring feelings of negativity or embracing positivity. This is not to say it is an easy task. It takes practice to accomplish and incorporate this kind of logic into our everyday lives. It takes the faith in God, self love, and a good heart to be able to implement these practices into our daily lives. But if you can do it, you will not only save yourself from health problems but you will benefit from peace of mind and the longer life you always wished for.

It is one thing to let go of those grudges, anger, and resentments, and it is another thing to leave some of them festering in your heart and hope for revenge. It is important to protect your mental health and stability. If you are unstable, you will not be able to see the dangers in front of you.

To free yourself mentally is to have no animosity, hurt or feelings of revenge each time you are around those who have hurt you. Most times, our mental state is what controls our health and entire physical body. When people are in a good state of mind, they are bound to do well in every area of our lives. The heart is important to our body, and so is our mental health. Our state of mind affects our emotional state.

People may tell those who wronged them that they have forgiven them but deep down they still feel pain and have it in their minds to seek revenge. If you are one of those people, you still have not freed yourself mentally from those who have wronged you. When you harbor such negative feelings, you are still mentally living in the prison protected by those that wronged you. You remain incarcerated in that prison if you beat yourself up when you hear about them, get angry when you see them, or have feelings of revenge towards them. Their actions against you are still controlling your mood and influencing your decisions. Your resentment and anger can affect many other innocent people, get you into big trouble that could jeopardize your life, or possibly end your existence in the world.

That is why it is imperative to mentally free yourself from this bondage and stop reacting to things out of the anger or frustration based on what people did to you. It is only when we free ourselves mentally that we can live happily and positively, contribute to the lives of people around us, and to society. It will also save us from health challenges throughout our lifetime.

When you decide to let go of the pain, agony, and the stress of weeping over the wrong people have done to you, do it wholeheartedly without any form of hidden spirit of revenge. Don't make the choice to live in the prison of your offender. When you completely let go of those things, you will enhance your life and get the full health benefits of a long life. Allowing resentment and anger to dwell in your heart is like inviting someone to place an unfair burden on you. Do not let someone else's misbehavior hold you prisoner.

It is also important to recognize that hate and resentment can live in your subconscious without you being aware of it. You may give off negative vibes through a frown or a negative attitude just because someone else wronged you. You must recognize that when you harbor negative feelings because someone has wronged you, it can affect your behavior towards others. Those negative vibes will also gradually destroy you without your knowledge. It is only when you get rid of those grudges that you can accommodate good feelings and a more positive spirit. Being free of negative energy will lead to a more peaceful life, free of mental health challenges. It is only when you free yourself from a prison of resentment and anger that you can live a fulfilled, long life.

CHAPTER SIX

LIVE IN THE PRESENT MOMENT AND EXERCISE REGULARLY

ONE OF THE things we can practice that will enable us to live longer is to dwell only in the present. When we live in the present, it will be hard to turn our minds, thoughts, and energy to things that are not relevant to us. If we are distracted by other worries, it will affect our well-being and health. This does not mean we should ignore different tasks in our daily routine. We should keep our minds open to other assignments. But by focusing on the task at hand, and not getting upset about things we cannot yet accomplish, we will keep at bay negative energy.

It is important to direct our focus, energy, and undivided attention towards what we can do in the present moment. Avoid distractions that can hurt your health. and channeling our energies in the present will guarantee we get the best out of what we do and out of our lives generally. You should learn to live your daily life as if there is no tomorrow. This passage in Matthew 6:34 provides guidance for us. "Take therefore no thought for the morrow: for the morrow shall take thought for the things of itself. Sufficient unto the day is the evil thereof."

In other words, we should not worry about tomorrow, for tomorrow will worry about itself. Each day has enough trouble of its own already. This does not mean you should not take care of your tomorrow. Instead, it means you must make your present moment your priority and that will be in the best interest of your health. Learn to live your best life in your present moment and give it your best effort. That way, you can build toward tomorrow knowing that you have completed the tasks in your present.

Do everything at your own pace and don't let stress desta-bilize your effort. Don't give in to depression which can gravely impact your life. Here is a good formula.

- Focus eighty percent of your efforts towards the present, and twenty percent on the future.

- Be optimistic that things are going to be fine.

- Focus on things you are doing at that moment.

- If you have things that make you happy, like new clothes, shoes, cars, and other things, use them.

- Do not save for tomorrow what will make you happy and comfortable today because when you are happy you will create positive energy.

People who do not live their best lives in their present moment do so because they are trying to save their best for tomorrow. Let's face it. No one knows what is going to happen in the next second, minute, hour, or day. Anything can happen. We see cases in the news everyday where people have left their homes and never came back to them. People die everyday in accidents, as victims of violence, and in natural disasters. Or they can find themselves in crossfire. When you prioritize what is happening in the present, you will experience the true essence of happiness in life. It is only when you are happy that you can concentrate on everything else around you. So, pay more attention when driving. Be aware of potential hazards around you. Follow the rules that govern society. Live to the best of your ability.

Channel all your energies towards what is happening in the here and now. Everyone has limited time on earth, so we should learn to live this time to the best of our abilities. Living your best life in the present will boost your immune system against potential health challenges.

Remember: you do not have to be extremely rich or have everything in the world to have the feelings of fulfillment. Having riches or wealth can not guarantee fulfillment in life. Try instead to make the best out of what you have, and you will feel a sense of achievement. Do not worry about tomorrow. Do not prioritize tomorrow. Focus on today. In that way, you will live your best life and safeguard your health. Living for today will give you peace of mind. It will brighten your day. It will give you positive feelings about your life.

Worrying about tomorrow has led people to commit desperate acts they could not have imagined. Living for the future does not add value to your life. It could even cut it short. Living for the future is a waste of your energy, particularly if you have not taken care of the present. Living for the future means you are giving it power over your present. Living for the future can lead to feelings of fear, panic and restlessness which will negatively impact your well-being. Living for the future can elevate your blood pressure, drain your positive energy, aggravate your stress level, and can disable your mental faculties. That is why it is imperative to stop worrying about the future and start managing what is directly in front of you. When we do that, we are not only freeing ourselves from the bondage and fear of our future, but we are also creating a healthy environment and enabling us live longer lives.

Exercising your body is a wonderful way to guarantee good health. Exercise feeds your body, your soul, and your well-being. It is an essential part of healthy living in our society today. Exercise will give you strength and prepare you to perform better on a day-to-day basis. Exercise will boost our body immune system and make it function more efficiently. Exercise builds our muscles, gets us into shape, and burns toxins from the body, and makes us healthier. Exercise makes our hearts beat faster and produce fresh blood. Exercise reduces mood swings, repairs our joints, and refreshes the mind. Exercise produces endorphins that fight off feelings of depression. when you are exercising, do it according to your strength, and remember, it is not how long you spent in the gym that gets you into shape. It is the consistency of exercising often by accommodating it in your schedule.

People often equate exercising with weight loss or reversing a medical condition but it does more than that. It is simply good for the body and will improve your health. We should not wait until we have issues, we should be pro-active and positive about exercise. We should not wait to start.

Exercise brings clarity to the mind. It refreshes our brain cells and memories, and it helps us function better. This is not to say incorporating exercise will be easy. We are all busy with our daily routines and starting an exercise regime will take effort. But it is possible to achieve. and you will see a difference!

Look at two people, one who exercises and one who does not. One is physically fit and is flexible. The other carries unnecessary pounds and can perform fewer physical tasks. The fit individual has stronger joints and greater mobility. The unfit individual will encounter problems in these areas as they age.

People who exercise regularly are more optimistic. They have better circulation and mobility. They reduce their risks for heart attacks, high cholesterol, high blood pressure, shortness of breath, cancer and other illnesses that can shorten their lives.

Regular exercise:

- improves your mood, and mental health.
- helps your sleep better.
- reduces depression.
- controls weight.
- reduces anxiety.

- enhances concentration.
- makes you feel and look younger.
- improves your sexual performance.

Try to condition yourself to exercise two to three times a week, and do not overdo it, especially when you first get started. Exercising too much can cause injury. As in everything in life, moderation is key. Consider exercise as a hobby that is good for you. Make a point of adding it to your calendar just as you would a medical appointment or a lunch date. If you embrace activity, you will reduce the toxins in your body, increase your life span and avoid health issues that plague older individuals.

CHAPTER SEVEN

LEARN TO SMILE AND BE HAPPY

THERE IS NOTHING more beautiful in the world than a person who is always smiling, and happy. People cannot help but want to join in and share their positive spirit. Smiling is infectious. When we are happy, we tend to excel in whatever we are doing. When we smile, we feel good and we positively impact others' feelings around us. Smiling reduces stress, makes us feel good, brings out our positivity, strengthens our hormones and brings out the best in us.

Our very lives depend on our happiness. If we are not happy, we are likely to make mistakes, do things we would normally not do, make wrong decisions, get angry easily, and make bad choices that can negatively impact our lives. Most times, happiness and smiles go together because when we are happy, our smiles come naturally. This is not something we have control over. It is just our body's natural response each time we are happy. A smile is like turning a light on whenever we are in a happy mood. Happiness always drags a smile along and boosts our energy in life.

Smiling and happiness will enrich the body, spirit, and soul. It will make your life blossom. Think of your smile as the sunshine, and your happiness as the rain. The sun energizes the plant while the rain gives it strength. Without the sun and the rain, the plant withers and dies. A person who lives without happiness has feelings of anger, resentment, stress, unhappiness, and bitterness. Constantly living an unhappy life will diminish your life, and health. Being happy, on the other hand, is a gift to yourself.

You should never expect other people to make you happy; you are the one who can create your own happiness. Do not allow yourself to depend on others before you can be happy; always learn to make yourself happy. Being happy, and always smiling will improve your quality of life, and you will influence people around you in positive ways. When you give someone a smile, you will trigger a positive feeling and reaction in them. If you smile at them, they will smile at you. When somebody is in a happy mood, their entire body system changes in a positive way which will, in turn, boost their immune system and make them healthier.

So, it is imperative to fill your soul by always smiling and being happy. You deserve it. Smile is contagious and each time you put a smile on someone's face, you get back the positive vibe right away. When you smile, it not only positively impacts your well-being, it also throws light on the lives of the people around you. The more you smile, the more you develop good feelings that will make you feel better all day.

Do not let your difficulties in life stop you from smiling. Constantly being in a bad mood will not be beneficial to your health. Instead, do everything you can to keep smiling and be happy no matter what life throws at you. You should never allow the world's troubles to silence your happiness and suppress your smile. Always try your best to find happiness, and your smile in every situation. Certain things are bound to happen in our lives, and we cannot always control or avoid these things. But we can control how we respond to them. This is not to say that controlling and responding to these negative situations in our lives is always an easy task, but if we are resilient, determined, and have a positive mindset we can meet life's challenges. If we look positively on every situation, we have a good chance of making things better. How we respond will determine the damage to us and others.

Do not invite people or circumstances into your life that will take away the better part of you. Beware of things that take away your smile and happiness, and do not give negativity any space in your life. Your smile and happiness are too important to compromise. You must do everything in your power to make sure you are in total control of your feelings. If you let tricky situations hinder your smile and happiness, you will let various health problems creep into your life. They will cause problems like high blood pressure, constant mood swings, depression, low self esteem, as well as other health challenges. These conditions will destabilize you and your overall well-being and place you in a vulnerable situation that may affect your life span.

Prioritizing your smile and happiness will attract more good things to you because positivity will play a key role in determining how long you will live on earth. Do not disregard their importance; it could further complicate and jeopardize your life. If you see a situation that could make you vulnerable, try to avoid it. It may severely affect your health. Choose your good physical and mental health instead. If you choose smiling and happiness, you will improve your well-being and add years to your life. Make them a priority. and always remember to guard your heart, and well being. Try to avoid becoming frustrated and overwhelmed by bad situations, lest they lead you to an early grave.

Finally, we must all learn to always be happy and smiling, and to incorporate safety techniques into our day-to-day activities that will strengthen our resolve and further guard us from many adversities in life.

CHAPTER EIGHT

BE POSITIVE AND
AVOID TOXIC PEOPLE

SURROUNDING OURSELVES WITH positive people can add value to life. They support us and help us live longer. But when we bring negative people into our orbit, they bring along negative baggage that will have the opposite effect. Do not let negative individuals add you to their social circles. Allow yourself the luxury of choosing who you let into your life. You know yourself better than anyone. You know the kinds of behavior you are willing to accept. So, you are in the best position to choose, or accept, friendships.

When you have positive people in your life, you invite positivity into your environment and good things will happen to you. By surrounding yourself with positive people, and adopting a positive attitude yourself, you will live longer, process information better, change the way you think and reason, and you will treat others in a positive fashion. When we accommodate positive minded people in our lives, we can excel in whatever we do and soar beyond our own expectations including in areas where we need improvement. Good things will come with this. Allowing positive minded people into our lives is like giving ourselves an extra ability to move our lives forward. When a positive person is in your life, their spirit and energy will creep into your heart. Their interests will now be your interests and their influence will change how you behave. Positivity is infectious, and you will want to do everything they are doing and follow their example in making decisions and choices. Their example will influence your happiness and success.

Let us say you accepted a friendship from a person you know is engaged in dubious activities. They are always in trouble. If you allow them into your space, they will drag you into their own mess and eventually steer you off the right path. That is not to say that people cannot change, but if they are on the wrong path, they will influence your life in a negative fashion.

Being around positive people will: increase your strength, make you feel good, pick you up when you are down, add to the quality of your life, lead you in the right direction, give you a reason to live and ease your pain and agony.

It is not easy to find positive people in our society, so if you are lucky to find one, hold them tight and never let them go. People with good mindsets can be your confidants when you get into trouble. They can take away your pain when you are unhappy and will always be available for you. They will brighten your spirit in dark moments by filling your soul with words of encouragement.

When you have positive people in your life, there are no bounds to your progress, and happiness. By their example, they will show you the way to a successful life. They will give you that little push, and give you what you need to breakthrough any difficulty, they will have your back when you are not there, and will make your life better with positive feelings and enhance your life. Toxic people should never enter your personal space if you want to live longer.

Toxic people will:

- bring out the worst in you.

- never see a good thing in whatever you do.

- find faults where there are none.

- always look down on you,

- never tell you the truth when you are wrong,

- get you in trouble.

- applaud you to your face and trash you behind your back.

You will always be able to spot a toxic person. They will give signs but sometimes a person is too blind to see them. They may be secretly jealous of you. They may sense that your future is brighter than their own. They may not possess the qualities that you have and decide they want to bring you down to make themselves feel better. They may use you to get ahead, or simply want your downfall at all costs.

It is important to avoid people who are constantly angry, people without integrity, people who have no respect for you, people who are dishonest, people who cannot add value to your life, people with no ambition to improve their own lives. It does not matter if they are family, friends, or acquaintances, just stay away from them. Do not let them cut you off from the people you care about and try to distance yourself gradually especially when the person is related or connected to your family.

You will have to apply wisdom in handling situations like this in order not to hurt their feelings or make them eternal enemies. Making enemies is not good for your mental health. Think logically about the situation before gradually pulling away. Be courteous and exchange greetings with them. But draw a line between you and them to ensure they do not have a negative impact on your life.

Toxic people play distinct roles in your life. They come to diminish you, to take good things and people away from you. Others come to isolate you from people in your life. Let us say you are a person who is doing well and is comfortable in life. The toxic person will try to make you uncomfortable, and you will begin to have negative feelings that make your life unhappy. You will become vulnerable to negative emotions that are detrimental to your health.

Or you meet someone who is a divider who comes into your life to separate you from the people who have helped you grow. Dividers will feed you with negative thoughts about other family members and friends especially the ones they know will help you excel in life. They will make your life miserable by hindering all the good things that could have made your life better. and when these good things are gone, you will start to lose confidence in yourself. You will begin to experience low self-esteem. You will constantly feel bad, angry, unhappy. Nothing will excite you anymore. Your life will start moving in the wrong direction and your health will suffer. A toxic person will target the most well-meaning individuals and get them into trouble. They are like shop-lifters who take their friends along for the ride. The good person may want to show their peers that they are capable of the crime, that they are not weak. Some people are in jail today because of the toxic people they allow into their space.

The influence of the toxic person is immensely powerful. They can invade your personal space, and negatively influence and shape the ways you do things. They will actually start to alter your character, and if you are not careful, you will land where you do not expect or belong. Today, there are millions of people out there who are crying and wishing they could turn back the hands of time to correct their mistakes just because of the influence of the toxic people they allowed into their lives.

At the extreme, those who succumb to the influence of toxic people land in jail and regret heinous crimes they have committed. Unfortunately, they remain behind bars for exceedingly extended periods of time and are unhappy all the time. They become prone to developing illnesses that could prematurely end their lives. That is why it is imperative to avoid toxic people whom we know will negatively impact the good choices we make and decisions we take in whatever we do.

Toxic people are not entirely to blame. God gives each of us the ability to choose our journey. It is up to you to decide what path you take. Simply recognize that the influence of certain people can alter your journey forever. The best way to avoid trouble is to avoid people who distract us and hinder our progress and purpose in life. Even family members can put you into situations you will later regret. It is better to reduce the number of people who come into your life, who bring negativity.

Remember: toxic people will: get you into trouble, hinder you from fulfilling your life's purpose, make you bitter and unhappy, and increase your vulnerability to illnesses that can end your life. If you let them go, you will create room for the right people to come into your life.

CHAPTER NINE

ADOPT THE SPIRIT OF GIVING AND NOT TAKING

IN ORDER FOR us to live longer in life, we must all learn to give more to those in need in the world. Giving and helping people in need will give you joy, happiness, and amazing feelings. There is no better feeling than knowing you had positive influence in another person's life. You do not have to be rich to give to others, you can give from the little you have. There is always enough to share with people around us.

Each time you give to other people, you can see the smiles on their faces. You ignite a new spirit in them that is contagious. You will feel an overwhelming joy in your heart which will in turn improve your health and overall well-being. Always try to make giving part of your daily routine. You do not have to give money or gifts. You can render a helping hand by providing some kind of service like holding the door for another person to go through or helping them carry a heavy load. That is also giving. So is helping someone across the street.

There are people out there who do not have the spirit of giving but when someone else shows them that kindness, they are likely to pay it forward to others. So, when we give, we are not just helping those to whom we give, we are also giving them the idea to practice that same gesture in their day-to-day lives. When we give, we show others that there are still people in the society who care about other members of society. Some people have given up on life and humanity believing that no one cares about them. But when they see you care, they realize that there is still hope for them in life, and it reminds them that there are still nice people in the world.

When you give to others, never expect to receive that same favor from them. It is only God who rewards a cheerful giver. When giving to others, do it with excitement, happiness, and good intentions. Your gift will be their smile, and the good feeling you get from helping another person. Giving will boost your emotional, mental and psychological energy to help you perform more positively throughout your daily activities. When you are doing well in your daily activities, your health will improve and will extend your life span.

Giving of yourself makes the world a better place. Your gift may seem small to you, but it can be a big blessing to the people who receive it. So do not assume your gift is too small and decide to withhold an offering. Giving is giving. You might be saving someone's life by giving something you consider little. No matter how small, others will appreciate your gift. So, give with excitement and confidence. Each time you give, you give a gift to yourself. Joy will engulf your entire being, and the positive feelings you get will help you live longer.

This does not mean that you should not accept gifts from others. Just make sure the gifts they give you come from their hearts and will not leave them with less. Taking from others who need more can cause you guilt and produce negative feelings because you know others have less. You should resist the urge to take from people especially when you know they have less than you do, and need more. Your actions could impact you negatively with feelings of guilt and vengeance from God that could end or jeopardize your life. There are people in the world today who have much less than you do, and they need more to survive. If you take from them, it can have a lasting spiritual impact on your life.

There are individuals who believe that taking from others will improve their lives and enrich them. They forget that the hands that giveth are more blessed than those that taketh, according to God's teachings. You should feel honored and blessed that you are able to give to the needy and that they find you worthy enough to be of assistance to them. Do not be the one who always wants to take from others. Adopt the behavior of giving more and taking less from humanity.

and each time you give to others, never expect them to give you back anything in return. Simply ask them to give back to humanity when they can do so. It is only when everyone begins to pay forward such favors to others that the suffering in the world will reduce. By putting your kindness out into the world, help begins to circulate, and people are happier. That will make you happy, too, knowing that you have made a positive impact on another person's life. Taking less from people will make those things you could have taken available to others who truly need them. Overall, taking less from people will make more things available to the needy in the society, which will give you better positive feelings that will improve your health and will make you live longer in life.

CHAPTER TEN

LOVE NATURE
AND LIVE A SIMPLE LIFESTYLE

NATURE IS ONE of the gifts God has given us. God, in fact, created nature to help humanity on earth. Being in nature can make us feel better, act better, and makes the world a more pleasant and suitable place to live. When you love nature, it loves you back. It gives you joy, happiness and the good feelings that can extend your life span in the world. The water we drink, the food we eat, our clothes, and virtually everything we use everyday are products of nature. These things are life's necessities; we all can never, ever live without them.

Not everyone loves nature, but everyone should give nature a chance. If you learn to love nature, you will realize that it will help you in so many ways. If you simply show your interest in loving nature, good things will come your way in your everyday life. For example, being at one with nature will calm you, and help with anger and other terrible feelings you may be experiencing. Each time you are angry, just take time to go to the park or to a river to experience their majesty. The fresh air that you will breathe in the park, or at the river side, or at the seashore is quite different from city air, or recirculated air in buildings and houses. Fresh air provides a relaxing sensation that will help you let go of anger, anxiety, low spirits and other negative feelings you may be experiencing. Living in a stale air environment makes people sick and depressed and shortens their lifespans. Nature can heal so many negativities in your life. Sometimes, take off your shoes and place your bare foots on the ground to feel the dust, lawns, water and air. When you do this, you will experience the natural sensations of the earth that will give you good feelings and strengthen your life.

Getting out into nature whisks you away from the negative. If you choose to spend your time in solitary places like parks or at the seaside, you will find your relaxation spot. Sometimes appreciating God's work of nature can give you hope and the good feelings that can increase your life span. The trees, plants, flowers, and other natural things around us make life more worth living. Remember, nature also produces the oxygen we all breathe on a daily basis. Without these sources of oxygen, we would have gone extinct. The more you appreciate and love nature, the better your life will be.

When we continue to appreciate and love the good things of nature, we will experience the good feelings and support we need to move forward and live longer. We will appreciate its role in keeping us alive, and that can boost our immune systems to make us live longer.

It is also important that we choose to live a simple lifestyle. The world today is full of competition; people want to be above others and want to show that they are doing better than other people. There is a focus on materialism which has caused a lot of problems in many communities; it has prompted many individuals to pursue criminal activity and other unhealthy ways of living. Turning to crime is not an answer. The lives of criminals do not usually end well, but opposite is the case when they change from their ways.

To live a simple lifestyle is to love the things you already have because when you love the things you have, you will always feel you have everything you need in life. You will always feel content when you love what you have; when you are not content with what you have the spirit of greed takes over. People live their lives wanting more. They forget that what they desire only feeds into their vanity. It is only stuff. and you cannot take it with you. We should all care more about our salvation and our souls. We need these two things more than material possessions.

By living a simple lifestyle, you can ensure you will have peace of mind at all times. By choosing the simple life, you will stop wanting things you already have. You will save yourself from becoming a restless spirit, and you will focus on what is important in life. You will live longer without the stressful feeling of always wanting more.

In life, we all have different visions, purposes, goals, potentials, and dreams. We are all here for different reasons. There is no need for competition. Everyone of us will shine at a different time. So, if your friends are doing better than you are now, it doesn't mean you are a failure; it simply means that your time to shine is not here yet. Do not feel impatient because people around you are doing better than you. It is not worth stressing over. Remember: God will let you know when your time has come to shine.

Think of it this way. All fingers are not equal. Some are shorter while others are longer. No two lives are the same, either. It is the way God made the world. So, live your life simply. If things are bad now, they will not be bad forever. Do not worry what the future holds and choose to live in the present. It is not about where we are now; it is about living a righteous simple lifestyle without any stress and believing in the promises of God for the future.

Living a simple lifestyle has proven to be the best way in whatever we do because it brings us to doing things that really matter and leaves out the things that do not matter from our lives.

Follow these simple rules:

- Go about your life doing the things you can do without stress, anxiety, or discomfort.

- Indulge in things when you can, at your own pace, when you can feel relaxed and stress-free.

- Do not worry about being unsuccessful, and do not despair because you believe good things are not happening when you want them to happen.

Living a simple lifestyle will not only prepare you positively for the things ahead of you, but will also reduce your stress and save you from other unhealthy ways of living life that could prematurely destroy you.

CHAPTER ELEVEN

EAT HEALTHY FOODS AND DON'T TAKE LIFE TOO SERIOUSLY

EATING HEALTHY IS one of the significant things you can do to determine how your life journey will play out. It is important to pay attention to the foods you eat, their ingredients, and the times you eat. Each plays a vital role in determining your overall health. Every food you put in your stomach is processed and transmitted to other organs to keep you alive.

You are the decision maker who will determine what you put into your body. To stay healthy, always listen to your stomach. If it is growling, eat something. If it is not, resist the urge to feed it. Your stomach will thank you. This may seem like simple logic, but people find it difficult to follow this advice. They eat because of stress, because of boredom, or because of cravings. But that is not what your stomach wants.

Each time you eat when you are not hungry, the food puts unnecessary pressure on your digestive system. When your digestive system is pressured, it will take more time for the foods to break down completely. That is the reason people get constipated and find it difficult to pass their wastes. Improper digestion and bowel problems can cause serious health issues and may take your life.

The more you eat, the more work you give to your digestive tract. Terrible things can happen. You can develop painful stomach ulcers, bowel blockages, sensitivities, and other illnesses that can be life-threatening. One strategy that has been used for the ages is to fast every month at least once or twice. Fasting allows the stomach to take a break and relax. It is not for everybody, especially people with medical conditions, but it is wonderful for many people because it gives your stomach a break to re-energize after days and days of rigorously processing food.

Knowing the foods we eat is especially important because our bodies react to certain foods differently. That is why people have negative reactions to certain foods they eat, and others may have no reaction at all to that same food. People have allergies to foods like nuts, which can be life-threatening to them while others can eat the same food with no reaction at all.

If you find difficulty consuming one food or another, it is best to have allergy tests, through a specialist, who will give you guidance on what foods to avoid. If you choose not to use the allergy test process, you can also figure out if you are allergic to certain foods by eliminating them from your diet one by one. It is especially important to be aware of what foods are causing you problems to avoid long-term illnesses. Individuals have died, fallen sick or have even become critically ill because of the food they consumed out of ignorance.

Bad foods can negatively impact your digestive system and require medical attention. Sometimes it takes the grace of God to survive this. Another thing to pay close attention to is the time between when you had your meal and the time you go to bed. The time during these two activities is very significant to your digestive system. After each meal especially solid foods, you should give yourself at least three hours for the foods to digest before going to bed. Otherwise, it may cause you pains, constipation and other uncomfortable stomach problems because of the improperly broken-down foods in your bowel. However, your foods may take longer to digest because of your metabolism, gender, or digestive issues. The bottom line is to give yourself reasonable time for proper foods digestion before retiring to bed.

There are other things that can lead to a bad stomach. We need to remember to make sure our environments are always clean to avoid food contamination and poisoning. It is only through cleanliness of ourselves and our environment that we can safely prepare our meals without any dangerous contamination that could endanger our lives.

Similarly, we must also be cautious of the foods we consume in restaurants where foods are not always properly handled and prepared. When possible, we should observe the cleanliness of the eateries and see how the chefs prepare our food. If they wash their hands, keep a clean kitchen, and ensure the ingredients are sanitary, we can safely eat what they offer.

We must also pay attention to the cleanliness of the stores where we buy our food. It is important to choose stores that place an emphasis on sanitary practices. It is up to you to choose what kinds of food you put into your body. It is also up to you to ensure that what you eat is clean, and safe. It is easy just to pick something up because you are hungry and forget about the cleanliness of its place of purchase. But we should make sure that all surfaces are clean, and food is prepared properly to ensure what we are eating is safe.

Sometimes, it is not possible to see how people prepare our food but we can at least visualize the environment in which these foods are prepared to ascertain if the foods are clean or not. We decide if we should eat certain foods, and so it is up to us observe the environment where our foods are prepared. Are those preparing the food wearing gloves and hair nets while handling the food? Does the server wash down the surfaces on a regular basis? Pay attention to these things to avoid dangerous contaminated foods that could place you on the verge of early death.

Food poisoning kills people around the world every day. That is why we must always apply caution before consuming foods especially the kind we did not handle ourselves.

You should never consume anything you know is unhealthy for your body to avoid stomach issues. You should also learn to say no to certain things you know will negatively impact your stomach. That is one key to a longer life.

Do not accept foods from people just to please them or just because it is free. You must learn to say no -- especially when you know the food will not be pleasing to your stomach. People accept food that is not good for their bodies because of ignorance, or low self-esteem. Others accept food from others not knowing the damaging effects it can cause their bodies. Always watch the kinds of foods you eat because whatever you eat will be processed by your organs and end up circulating through various parts of your body.

Many individuals do not have the confidence to reject foods they know can affect their health. So, when they are given these foods by friends, family, or acquaintances, they take it just to please the giver. and because they do not know how to say no, they will end up consuming the foods that are obviously detrimental to their health..

Learn to say no to the foods you know are not healthy for you. Simply be polite in your refusal and give good reasons why you are refusing it. It may sound awkward to the giver if you stand your ground and do not accept their offer, but deep down you are trying to save yourself from something that may affect your life. Make them understand your situation, your allergic condition and why you are rejecting the food. Do not accept the food because it will make your host feel better. You are in charge of making decisions that will save your life. Avoid foods that are not healthy for you and try to always balance your diet.

It is also important to factor in age when it comes to food consumption. As you age, you become more sensitive to certain kinds of food, and will benefit by limiting their consumption. As you get older, you should be more selective about what you put into your mouth. You know what you should and should not eat based on how that food makes you feel inside. With age comes wisdom, and awareness that will save you from consuming foods that could be disastrous for your health.

As we grow older, the internal organs in our bodies will become weaker and weaker. The way our organs processed foods when we were in our teens and twenties is not the same way they process them when we are above forty years of age. You must limit the consumption of certain foods at a certain age and stage to avoid chronic health conditions. If you want to live your life without medication, you should learn to balance your diet by adding in more fruits and vegetables. Try to add natural ingredients like garlic, ginger, lime and other traditional ingredients when preparing your meals because they have been proven to have health benefits for the human body.

If you have not already started adding natural ingredients to your diet, you may not like the taste of them, at first. But you should consider their health benefits and try to use them as often as you can if you are not allergic to them. Using natural foods will help strengthen your internal organs, clean your stomach lining, strengthen your veins, improve your digestive system, and purify your blood stream. If you cannot add natural ingredients to your cooking because others in your household have allergies, you can always try drinking them in tea, shakes and smoothies. You will get the same health benefits regardless of how you consume them.

We must all learn to choose wisely when it comes to the foods we consume, and to treat ourselves to nutritious foods that are good for our bodies. The bottom line is that the foods you feed your body will determine how healthy and sound you will become in your lifetime journey.

Colon health is also vitally important. One easy way to keep it clean is to consume water on an empty stomach when you wake up in the morning. Water consumption on an empty stomach in the morning has proven to be highly effective in the cleaning up of your colon and digestive system in so many ways. There are individuals who may not know this but it is a terrific way of eliminating unwanted particles from our stomach lining and colon. It will improve your digestive system and free you from constant constipation, stomach-aches, stomach grumbling and other chronic health issues that could gradually destroy your life. Drinking water on an empty stomach will clean up your guts and refresh your entire body system, and make you feel better and happier. If you do not flush and clean your system on a regular basis, you can develop terrible illnesses over your life span.

Another grave mistake is holding yourself instead of visiting the bathroom. Holding wastes back will do you more harm than good. It doesn't make you stronger; in fact, it can gradually cause serious damage to your digestive system.

People today take themselves too seriously. We all need to realize life will not always be a bed of roses. One thing can happen this minute, and something totally different can happen the next minute. You must learn to accept these things when they happen. Think of life as a series of weather patterns. One day it rains, the next minute the sun shines and dries it up. When things happen in your life, never assume the worst. This kind of thinking will affect your overall health and could lead to more serious health conditions that may end your life. The best life strategy is to stop worrying over every little thing. Sometimes these things are meant to happen so that we can learn from them. Learning from our tragedies and reversals of fortune will make us stronger emotionally, mentally, and psychologically.

When something happens, keep an open mind. Do not take life too seriously, otherwise, you will end up hurting yourself and feel disappointment, anger, pain, and stress.

- Do not dwell on what you cannot change. You must learn to remain calm in every situation.

- Never assume the worst has happened to you. What you might think is the worst could end up as the beginning for other people.

- Do not be disappointed if you work towards something and you cannot get it.

- Do not stress out. Just keep in your mind that things will get better someday.

Say you are looking for a job, and you go in for an assessment or interview. You think you did well but the recruiter decides not to move your file forward. Try not to get upset or be angry over it. Try to accept the situation the way it is. The fact your application is rejected does not mean you did not do well, or your skills were not good enough, or you were not suited for the job. The recruiter might just have overlooked your fine qualities. They might have decided instead to choose another person because of their own personal interest. Or this is not the path God wants for you. Try to keep an open mind, and do not feel hurt if things turn out differently than what you wanted. It happens to everybody. Sometimes doors close right in your face. Sometimes, people will say you are not good enough. Do not let that pull you down and make you feel bad. Do not invite anger, regret, and stress into your life.

When you are stressed, you are bound to lose focus and go off track which will not be good for your life. So, each time you experience such difficulty, get up, dust yourself off and forge on. There will be better days ahead of you. If you do not take life so seriously, you will be able to overlook things that could have placed you in negative position in life. How you react does not have any effect on life itself. Your life will go on despite one disappointment. But you can change how you react and reduce the negativity in your life.

Whatever you experience or come across in life, accept it as it is and never take life too seriously no matter the situation. Having a cheerful outlook will allow you to live a healthy long life that will enrich your body and soul. Taking life too seriously will invite in negative feelings and stress that can gradually take over your health, and life. So, live your life the way it is, accept whatever comes your way without any stress or regret and do not let your emotions take over your sense of reason. You may regret it in later life. When you learn not to take life too seriously, you will:

- know how to navigate every situation.

- work hand-in-hand with other people.

- handle situations more carefully.

- feel no regret when people turn you down.

- have more confidence.

- tread more cautiously throughout your life journey.

CHAPTER TWELVE

_____

WISH OTHERS WELL AND BE AT PEACE WITH YOURSELF

YOU HAVE HEARD the old saying: what goes around comes around. It is true. Whatever you wish for others in life will come back to you. If you wish people well, good things will naturally come to you, but if you wish terrible things you will receive them in return. When your good wishes eventually come back to you, they will re-energize and strengthen your health and help you live a longer better life. Knowing that you have done the right thing by wishing others well will give you feelings of fulfilment and peace that will help you to move forward.

The life coach Tony Robbins has this advice.

"Always wish people well including those who have wronged you knowingly and unknowingly". It is understandable that this will be a hard practice for many individuals who would not want to incorporate it into their daily lives, but they need to do it and not just to do it alone, but also to have faith and believe that whatever good they wish others will come back to them in one way or the other.

"Whatever you believe, you can achieve."

Let's say a friend, acquaintance or colleague has offended you badly and you decide to hold it against them. Whenever you think of them, you have feelings of anger, frustration, and disappointment. You begin to feel stress, and that stress leads to depression. Your depression can then lead to chronic health problems that are life threatening.

What if you decide to manage the situation differently? What if you decide instead to forgive the person who wronged you and harbor no resentment towards them? When you forgive people who have wronged you and wish them well, it will give you the inner peace of mind that will positively boost your feelings and improve your overall health.

Wishing people well is not a sign of weakness. It is a way to make the world a better place for everyone. See it as a way to positively impact others, and protect yourself from unnecessary emotions, stress, and other negativity that could jeopardize your life. If you look at it another way, wishing people well will add to the positivity in the world. It can make life better for others, and it will bring joy and happiness into your life.

Life itself is full of struggles, and we do not need to add to the struggles of others. You know how it feels when others recognize your struggles. You feel relief right away, and their trust in you revives your trust in humanity. If you turn that around, and do the same for others, the world will be a less stressful environment in which to live. It is not realistic to assume that you can extend good wishes to everyone in the world. But the little you can do will make a significant difference especially when those you wish well would pay the favor forward. These feelings will circulate around the world in no time.

If you wish people well, you will reap personal benefits, you will feel less stress, you will be happier, and your actions will help make the world a more liveable place for all humanity. Try to be at peace with yourself. It is not always easy. Many people still struggle with this concept, and that struggle steers them away from their vision, dreams, and aspirations. Without inner peace, it is difficult to move your life forward, and stay healthy. What does inner peace mean? It means calming yourself and trying not to worry. It means forgiving yourself for all your trespasses now, and in the past. Everyone has made mistakes; everyone wishes they could have done things differently. Everyone has wronged others. It is human nature.

Yet many people have difficulty forgiving themselves and continue to flog themselves over things in the past even if their mistakes were made out of ignorance. There is no way you can be at peace with yourself if you fail to forgive yourself over things that happened in your early life. Mistakes pile up over time. It is understandable that things that happened in the past are hurtful, but we can not turn back the hands of time now to fix them. If that were possible, we would have tried to change things.

Since it is impossible to correct our past, there is no point in continuing to beat yourself up over the things that happened in it. All you will be doing is affecting your health.

Dwelling in the past:

- affects your mental health and leads to bitterness, frustration, anger, and extreme stress that can badly hurt your well-being.

- affects your daily performance and can lead you to making more mistakes.

- allows in negative thoughts that can determine how we will feel mentally.

- can make you feel unstable.

- can make you feel unsafe.

The more we are at peace with ourselves, the better our health and overall well-being. It is only when we are peaceful with ourselves that we can meet our full potential and live a long life. If you achieve inner peace you will work with integrity, work well with others, and humble yourself. If you cultivate the habit of wishing others well and being at peace with yourself, you will be able to enjoy the full essence of life and see all the beautiful things in it that will enhance your life.

Do not judge yourself by what others think of you. Too many people make this mistake. The only person who can add value to your life is you, so be the first to appreciate yourself and disregard what others think of you.

Eleanor Roosevelt once said, "no one can make you feel inferior, without your consent."

It is your choice to give people the power to use against you. Do not share with people what you do not like about yourself. They may try to judge you based on what you have told them. You must be mindful of the things you say about yourself. Even if you have physical challenges, do not look down on yourself, or bring yourself down in front of other people. Learn to always love yourself the way you are because that is the only way you can be at peace with yourself.

You choose how people will see you. If they see you as a rug, they will step on you. If you see yourself as lower than others, they will feel themselves above you. But if you see your own value, others will see it, too. They will respect you. They will value you. and when you are respected by others, it will bring out the best in you, and create a lasting calmness within you. You will be at peace with yourself.

When you are at peace with yourself, stress will be far from you, sickness will be far from you, and you will begin to live a healthier life. Love yourself the way you are and never allow anyone to reduce your value. No matter how you look, still elevate yourself and do not bring yourself down. You did not create yourself, God did. So, you must learn to appreciate who you are and what you look like. Feel comfortable under your skin, feel confident with your color, admire your ethnicity, and respect your own humanity. It is only when we place value on ourselves that others can see our worth. If you recognize your own value, and when others value how good you are, you will begin to feel a calmness and peace that will encompass your entire body. So, try everything within your power to be at peace with yourself. You will live longer.

CHAPTER THIRTEEN

DO THE THINGS YOU LOVE AND LIVE EVERYDAY AS IF IT WAS YOUR LAST

ONE OF THE best things we can do for ourselves is to do the things that we love. People do things every day that they do not like because of peer pressure, competition, or financial gain. They work at jobs that they do not like rather than finding a different path towards the things they love to do. What people fail to realize is that when we do the things we do not love to do, it directly affects our mental health. Imagine waking up in the morning to go to work you do not love. It will affect the way your day is going to play out. It will affect the environment in which you work. It will affect you psychologically and place your mental health at risk. You will begin to feel uncomfortable, angry, and unhappy, and these situations can negatively impact your life. There is nothing as good as when you go to a job you love; you feel happy, excited, and comfortable. These feelings strengthen your immune system, make your brain relax, energize you and make you feel healthier.

You should not engage in any activity you know is detrimental to your health just because somebody else is doing it. Everyone of us is unique in life. You must follow a path that makes you happy to wake up every day. There are many jobs to choose from. Try to find one that makes you happy, one that you love doing. Just because your friend is a nurse, a doctor, or an engineer does not mean you should choose their path. Everyone of us has things we are good at and things that we are not good at. Working hard at something you are not good at will cause stress. and when you are stressed out, you put pressure on your body, and your behavior starts to change and negatively affects your health.

Doing what you love will save you from many things that could destroy or cut your life short. Stress begins with the unimportant things, and the trivial things become bigger. Before you know it, those stressors begin to affect your health. Do things that make you happy, do things that give you joy, and do things that will bring out the positive feelings in you. It is only when you have positive feelings in you, that your psychological and mental health can be stable enough to efficiently carry you through your day-to-day activities. When your emotional, psychological, and mental health are negatively affected, and not stable, you will gradually begin to have health problems that may destroy your life. No matter what you do, always engage yourself in doing the things you love because that is one of the ways that will make you live a life of fulfilment.

Do not forget to live your life as if this day is your last. You should always enjoy yourself and take care of yourself in every conceivable way if you want to live your best life. It is only when you live your best life that your body will be strong and nourished, and you will live longer. You should always treat yourself in the best conceivable way. Taking care of yourself is your primary responsibility. It will determine how long you will live. Treat yourself to the things that will make you feel good and pleasant. Buy yourself good things, and whatever you feel you need.

If you think your spirit deserves something, and you can get it, go for it. Do not live a life where you deny yourself the good things in life, the things that make you feel better. Look for things that will minimize your stress. There is no point in being uncomfortable or waiting until there are no more problems in the world before you try to get what you want. Even God says the world will always have problems. You should live your best life because that is the best path to a long life.

You have to realize that we can not control things happening in the world, but we can definitely control how we react to them. You can live your best life by:

- always putting a smile on someone's face and watching them light up.

- doing things with integrity because you know you have done the right thing.

- surrounding yourself with people who love you for who you are, and not because of what you can give them.

- treating yourself to a nice vacation guaranteed to provide you comfort.

- loving yourself, and your life, and not comparing yourself to others.

Even if others are doing better than you, do not let it get to you, or allow it to negatively impact your life. Always see yourself as a successful person, and never look down on yourself because life is not about how much you make, it is about what you make out of the little you have.

At the same time, we must temper our lives, and not succumb to greed and jealousy. We should not live our lives constantly looking for more and spending every cent on things we do not need. Our insatiable quest for more can take us down a terrible path and can lead to problems with our physical, mental, psychological, and emotional well-being. Not everyone will survive the negative effects of always wanting more.

We must all learn to sew our coats according to our sizes to avoid unnecessary stress that will jeopardize our lives. Remember, it is the things we allow into our lives that will determine how our lives will play out. If we decide to live our best lives, we will get the best out of them, and if we decide to place ourselves in uncomfortable positions, that is exactly what we will get. Every one of us is capable of making these choices, so why not choose the path that will enhance your life instead of the one that will endanger it? Overall, living our best lives will not only boost energy, it will give each of us a better happier feeling, and increase our existence on this planet earth.

CHAPTER FOURTEEN

CHECK YOURSELF REGULARLY AND ADHERE TO DOCTORS RECOMMENDATIONS

BECAUSE YOU ARE responsible for your own health, it is important to get yourself checked out regularly by a doctor who may send you for tests after examining you in their office for signs of illness. Both are important because diseases will go undetected without proper testing. Never ignore any pains in your body no matter how little they might seem. A little pain can grow bigger and take your life if not treated on time. The moment you discover any pain or lump on any part of your body, let your doctor know right away.

Do not ignore these issues because if you wait, it could cost you your life. You don't know what the pains or lumps mean so it is important to consult your doctor in case something needs urgent attention. Too many people wait until their conditions worsen. By the time they get to the doctor's office, they are in excruciating pain. After the doctor orders tests, he discovers that pain is cancer, and that it has spread throughout the body. How would you feel knowing that you made the decision to see your doctor later, and that you have put yourself in more danger with a serious illness that could end your life? How would you feel knowing that the whole thing could have been avoided?

Always:

- observe your physical condition and examine your body when taking a shower or exercising.

- pay close attention to parts of your body that are feeling funny or in ways out of the ordinary.

- consult your doctor when you find something that feels uncomfortable.

- get the appropriate tests and scans.

You would not want to be in a situation where you will now be helpless in your condition and live a life of regrets. As the saying goes: "a stitch in time, saves nine".

The good news is that you can avoid unnecessary pain and illness if you take care of it on time. Never ignore any pains around your body especially ones you feel in your core where your internal organs reside. That is the area from your neck down to your waistline. This is your body's central command station that oversees sending fluids to the rest of your body. The body is like a car, and your core is like the engine. If anything goes wrong with that engine, your body will not move. So, take care of your core, and do not wait to report any negative medical concerns.

Aside from reporting any problems to the doctor, it is important to follow doctors' orders. People who refuse to listen to their doctors can find themselves in danger. Do not forget, your health does not just affect you. It affects your whole family. At times, people prefer to leave their health in God's hands. They think that if they believe in God, nothing will happen to them. It is true that God has the power to do anything in the world because He created it. But He also gave us free will to do what we need to do in the world to survive. He gave us the power to choose and decide.

So, it is up to you to choose good health, to get to the doctor when you are sick, to take the tests that may save your life and to follow doctors' orders. You cannot hide behind your religious beliefs. It is up to you to put out the effort before God can help you. That is why taking proper care of ourselves should be our top priority. Doing your part means running those tests and taking those medications. Doing your part means collaborating with God, and your doctors, to ensure you continue to enjoy good health. God could help you, but you are not in charge of God. The "grace of God," is not up to you.

and because He has given you the ability to make certain choices and decisions concerning your life, so He expects you to give him something to work with. People who solely rely on God for decisions they could have made on their own to enhance their lives have ended up six feet under because of their own carelessness. It is up to you to make the decision whether to follow your doctor's advice and recommendations. That is the power God has given to everyone.

God has given you power to make choices:

- You can choose to drink and drive and ruin your life.

- You can choose to marry someone with criminal traits who will put your life in danger and convince you to make bad choices.

- Your can choose to ride with a drunk driver and endanger your life.

- You can choose to cross the road against a light and take the chance a car will not hit you.

- You can choose to smoke and drink excessively and destroy your lungs and liver.

- You can also choose to ignore these bad choices and adopt upright way of living by making better choices that will be more beneficial to your life.

We all must be careful when making decisions daily. There is no doubt that drunk and distracted drivers and people who do not follow the rules and regulations cause accidents and death. But often human error causes road accidents when someone uses bad judgement. We should all learn to be more cautious when doing things in the world. We should not always expect God to protect us from the dangers we can see for ourselves because he often protects us from things we cannot see.

Since God protects us from the dangers we can not see, He expects us to tread carefully and avoid the dangers we can see. It is like following doctors' orders. Learn to develop the habit of making the right choices and decisions that will positively enhance your life. Always remember that we must show some effort in securing our own safety and life before leaving the rest for God to complete.

CHAPTER FIFTEEN

TRAIN YOUR POSITIVE MIND TO OVERCOME YOUR NEGATIVE MIND

ONE OF THE things we can incorporate into our daily practice is allowing our positive minds to overpower our negative minds. We all have negative and positive minds that compete against each other. Your positive mind makes choices that positively impact your life while your negative mind keeps feeding you negative self-talk. When your positive mind is speaking to you, it presents you with scenarios that will show you what you will gain from dealing with an issue in a positive manner. When the negative mind speaks, it is more complicated. Your negative mind will not always fill you in on the consequences of acting badly. It will simply show the rewards of your negative action.

It is only after you have done the wrong thing that you will see the gravity of what you have done. That is why people show remorse after negative actions. Saying that you did not know what you did was wrong does not excuse your actions. Sometimes, people know exactly what they are doing. But sometimes, your negative mind can trick you into believing that what you are doing is the right thing.

Making decisions using your positive mind leads to greater feeling of joy, happiness, and excitement that will direct you to the right path in life. Thinking with your negative mind will bring you feelings of anger, resentment, animosity, and other negativities that will place you in danger that could destroy your life. That is the reason someone who acts with their negative mind regrets their actions because when people are angry or have a spirit of resentment, they do not have the ability to reason appropriately. Negative thoughts can cloud their sense of reasoning. Sometimes, an individual denies their actions after they come to their senses. They begin to sob and weep after they realize they could have handled things differently.

As human beings, we are all structured and wired to think in positive or negative directions. When we are walking, standing, sitting, running, or doing other activities, there is always something on our minds. People struggle between making good and bad choices daily. There are people who can easily choose their positive thoughts over their negative thoughts, and there are people who allow their negative thoughts to always overcome their positive thoughts. The people who lack control and allow their negative thinking to take over their positive thinking are those who gets in trouble all the time. Eventually, following their negative thoughts will get them in big trouble. They will violate the laws, and take them on a negative path.

People often wonder why certain individuals always get in trouble wherever they go. The reason usually is that they allowed their negative minds take over their positive minds. There is no way that positive and negative thoughts do not cross our minds. A person is guided by their instincts and their senses: sight, hearing, smell, taste and feel. They make different assumptions based on those senses, and they will begin to run through positive and negative thoughts.

The good news is that God gave us the power to decide and wants us to use our own discretion to make our choices and decisions instead of following our basic instincts. If you ask, God will help you, leading you to a path of truth and spirit. He will come in to guide you through that perilous process to make the right decision that will give you the good feelings of peace which will prolong your life. People who serve God in truth and in spirit wholeheartedly understand His likes and dislikes and will be able to make the right decisions that will not negatively affect them.

The Book of Genesis talks about the issue of human creation. That is where positive and negative minds originated from. After God created everything in the world, He created us in His own image, and gave us the responsibility to make decisions so that we would be able to take total control over other creations on earth. After He created humans, He designated an area in the Garden of Eden and gave instructions to Adam to eat every other fruit in the garden except a particular one. What does this tell us? This implies that when God was creating us, He created in us the ability to make choices, decisions and follow instructions. That is why he specifically instructed Adam not to eat that fruit in the garden.

God wanted Adam to be able to differentiate between the good and the bad. Adam was able to adhere to these instructions until Eve decided to violate God's orders by eating the forbidden fruit after the serpent deceived her. Even after Adam relayed God's instructions to Eve, her negative mind still overcame her positive mind to disobey God thanks to the bad influence of the serpent. The serpent's role was to create the negative mind in human beings, and that is why we all think about the good things as well as the bad things.

The positive mind is that of God while the negative mind is that of the serpent devil. Your positive mind speaks to you at the same time as your negative mind also speaks to you. The good part is that we all have that ability to choose between the two minds. People who choose to listen more to their negative minds always end up getting in trouble and doing things that will negatively affects their lives. It is that same negative mind that allows people to make dangerous choices and decisions that will abruptly terminate their lives and send them to their early graves. So, if your wish or goal is to live a peaceful longer life, you must choose the thoughts of your positive mind over the negative mind.

You know the difference between the good and the bad. You know the impact the good mind has on your life in the same way you know about what the negative mind can do. That is why it is important to choose integrity in your everyday life. It will prolong your existence. Some people believe they can secretly do negative things and get away with them. That is their negative minds clouding their sense of reasoning. It is human nature to reflect on things using both your negative and positive minds.

How do you train or control your positive mind over your negative mind? You do so by knowing God and serving Him in truth and in spirit. Follow His commandments and apply those commandment instructions to your life's journey. The commandments vividly outline the things you should not do.

Ask yourself: What would God do if He were in your situation? A true believer in God will always pause to think and reason before acting on any situation that comes their way. During that pause, they will reflect on the question, and produce a solution. But if you do not worship Him in truth and in spirit, your negative mind will likely overcome your positive mind and lead you on a bad path that could terminate your existence on earth.

You must know how to use the ways of God to manipulate your negative mind because anyone who has the fear of God will apply his commandments to their daily life practices. In the ten commandments, God lays out the things you shouldn't do and consequences you will face if you violate His words of wisdom. When you obey God and fear those consequences, you will positively shape your mind and do the right thing. But if you refuse to fear those consequences and continue with your negative lifestyle, you will start to make wrong choices and decisions that will land you in grave situations that could abruptly end your life existence in the world.

CONCLUSION

HOW YOUR LIFE will turn out will rest on your relationship with God. That relationship affects the things you engage in, the choices you make and the decisions you take every moment of your life. It is your choice whether to follow the rules of life that navigate how far you will go in life.

It is often said that whatever we put out to the world will always find a way of coming back to us. When we put positive things into the world, positive things will naturally come to us, and when we put negativity into the world, that will also determine what we will get in return. So, it is imperative to always take the positive approach in life to get the best out of it. Life is full of choices and decisions, and it is good, and in our best interest, to always stop and think before making those choices and decisions. The choices we make, and the decisions we take, always play a paramount role in determining our life existence. Every one of us knows the difference between the good and bad in life, and we all have the capability given to us by God to choose between these two. Sometimes, we cannot completely stop negative thoughts from coming into our minds, but we can certainly control how we react or respond to those thoughts. Similarly, we cannot stop things from happening to us, but we can change how we react to these things.

The choices and decisions we take in life could either enhance or terminate our existence on earth. That is up to everyone of us. We can choose to be grateful and content with the things we already have, the lifestyles we choose to live, the people we allow into our space, our decisions to appreciate the things we have, and many other things. We should always remember that God has given us a reasonable amount of control over our lives so it is up to us to consider those choices wisely. We must be cautious in making our choices and decisions so as not to bring negativity into our lives. If we take a positive approach as we live day-to-day, we will live much longer. and we must all play a role as part of humanity and leave the rest to God to complete.

In the previous chapters, we have discussed the importance of living a productive positive way of life, the dos and don'ts and how we can apply these positive lifestyle choices to our daily activities. We have learned that sometimes we can be under the influence of people who go against the positive way of life. These individuals will try to stop the good things you are trying to do or have done; they will try to take you backwards and to make you believe that doing the wrong things are better than the right ones by trying to change your mindset. They will try to entice you with materials and worldly things to win you over to their side.

People are particularly vulnerable when they try to change their negative ways. They may start to backslide and start doing the wrong things again. If they are strong, and refuse, rebuke, and bluntly reject those advances and stand their ground during that critical time, they will be able to reap the fruits of their honorable deeds and live longer. But if they give in to the negative and tricky ways of those negative influencers, then they will find themselves getting in trouble that could destroy their own existence on the planet.

It is important to always follow the word of God by constantly reading the Bible and adhering to its teachings while using good energy to take care of your mind, body, and soul for the benefit of humankind. When you are possessed by positive energy and the word of God, you will be at your best and you will create an environment that will benefit you and others in the world in a spiritual and healthy manner. Each time we follow the word of God, positive spirits will take over our lives and it will show in our behavior towards others. We will begin to develop a better attitude that will help us do the right things that will prolong our lives. Once we have the right attitude, we will enjoy love, peace, harmony, happiness, and other good feelings. We will also begin to use our positive feelings to help other people for the benefit of all humanity. So, having God's presence in our lives and the right attitude towards life will not only make us live longer but it will also ease the problems in the lives of people around us.

When we have a good relationship with God, we will be able to follow life's rules and instructions and things will begin to fall into place. But when we do not know our position with God, our lives will become unstable. Just remember that we do not always get what we want or expect. Perhaps that path is one that God does not want for us. We must be patient and allow things to naturally happen. It is best not to force the situation to our own advantage. Otherwise, we could land in trouble.

Overall, what we must understand is that if we make wrong choices, decisions, and mistakes, it can shape and mold us in the wrong direction. We should not allow bad choices to define who we really are. Every human being has that good part in them, and we must do everything humanly possible to bring out the best in ourselves, and to relinquish any bad behaviors that put us in trouble or endanger our lives. That is why God declares in His words that no matter how big our mistakes and sins in life are, He will still accept us the way we are. He will purify our minds, bodies and souls if we can wholeheartedly repent from those sins and believe in Him. When we believe in Him, we will experience calmness of the mind, cleanliness of the body, purification of the soul, and our good choices and decisions will enrich our lives, uplift us up, and give us what we need to strengthen ourselves and allow us to live longer in life.

ACKNOWLEDGEMENTS

I am grateful to God for creation of this book and for the writing, editing, formatting, and publishing that will make it a success. Thanks to my precious immediate family for the significant role they play, and how they have supported my journey. I want to thank my editor and her team for their role in making this book achieve its desired purpose. All the events described in this book are real; they accurately represent the things everyone can incorporate into their lives to enhance them.

The Bible verses come from the King James version, both online and hard copy.

ABOUT THE AUTHOR

BRIGHT DESTINY OSAIYUWU is a writer, motivator, philanthropist, mentor, security professional, life and spiritual coach. Bright was born in Edo-State, Nigeria, in the western part of Africa, and is currently living in Toronto, Canada, with dual citizenship. He had his early education in Nigeria and post-secondary education in Canada. The author's mission is to mentor, inspire, motivate, and encourage his readers and listeners to help to improve their way of living. His life experiences and observations of things that happen to human beings in the world prompted him to write this book in hopes that everyone can incorporate these teachings into their lives and enhance them.